His Eyes are Open Wide

P. T. Lewis

Library of Congress Control Number: 2012903986

ISBN:	Hardcover	978-1-4691-7819-6
	Softcover	978-1-4691-7818-9
	Ebook	978-1-4691-7820-2

This book was printed in the United States of America.

To order additional copies of this book, contact:
Xlibris Corporation
1-888-795-4274
www.Xlibris.com
Orders@Xlibris.com
69386

CONTENTS

Sometimes we live our whole life doing what we know is not right. When we get hit upside the head, then we begin to listen. We have to be totally broken for the father to use us. The father has to wash all the pride out of us. Slay all of our bad habits. That can be a process. You know how you tried to quit smoking. You quit one week or a month and started back. You must ask the father to take it away for good. You must ask the father to take the desire out of your mouth. Then you have to deal with your fifthly mouth. They say the tongue is the dirtiest thing on you. The words that come from your mouth cut like a two edge sword. God has to crucify that part of us too. When the lord gets through, we find that we are apologizing to others for what we said to them. We are kinder to people. The father just wants us to be like him. If he is going to put his spirit in you, sooner or later you will change or die. You can live long on this earth, are you can choose the short path death. God gives us a choice free will. Just like all the people that have died in the graveyard. They had a choice, they did not want to step into the kingdom. They decided to live there life anyway. That is why they are no longer with us. We all have a short time on this planet to get are life right. When your number is up, there is nothing else you can do. We are in this beautiful world to solve a problem. God did not create us to just take up space. We must be about our father business. The father gives us plenty of time to make up our mind. Then he pulls us out of it.

Sometimes we are left here to be a witness and sometimes we are taken away. We all have to use are time wisely. One thing for sure is that you will never get the years back that you wasted in your life. These bodies we have will grow old someday. That is why we must take full advantage of our youth. Have the family that god so wants you to have. Let's stop being selfish and take care of our babies that god gives us. If God has given you children they are very special to him. Let's not mistreat them. My father does not like anyone to hurt the children. Now parents please try to not party with the children. How can you raise a child to respect you, when you want to party with that child. The children in your life are a blessing from God. We must cherish them and provide for their needs. We are our children's first teacher, they watch their parents. Now if your child sees you smoking or drinking, what do you think they will do. If your child see's mom or dad cussing all the time, what do you think they will do. We as parents cannot wait until little Johnny is 18 to try to correct him. If you let him talk to you any kind of way when he is young. When he gets older he'll probably knock you out. If we train up a child when they are young, they want depart to much from it when they get older. This one pastor said, some of the pastors children are the worse ones. If the pastors would take time for their children, just like they take time for church activities. Then maybe the children would be different. If your children don't get any attention from you or your wife. They will go other places to get attention. We must be street smart as well as book smart.

The next day I and my children went to the grocery store. This mother was cussing at her children just because they wanted some candy. I said excuse me! Do you have to cuss them out? I will buy them what they want. She said listen they are my kids I will talk to them anyway I want. I told her God gave you those kids. He did not give you the children to abuse them. If you are having some problems I can pray for you now. She just broke down and started crying. So I started to pray for her. She was worried about her bills and how she was going to feed her children. So after I got through praying for her I told her about resources that could help her out with her needs. She was so glad that I gave her knowledge about her situation. Many times we don't know why people do the things they do. When a person is hurting they will hurt other people. If we could heal all the mother's in the world, we have just saved their children from child abuse or worse. The father is supposed to be the provider. Today society is different, we have mother's that are raising girls and boys. The mother is the provider in the household. The child has only one parent to look up too. This brings a lot of emotional stress, down on the mother's shoulders. The mother prays every day for strength and guidance to raise her children. Some mothers have a support system, and some do not. A good mother tries to find father figures to mentor her sons. Some things women cannot teach a boy, is how to be a man. At the same time if a woman does not have any one to help her, she has to try to do the best that she can. Many times a mother goes to sleep crying, because sometimes the load just gets so hard to bare.

God wants to move his children into the super natural realm. In order to get to this level in Christ you must hunger and thirst for him. Only when you hunger and thirst for him will you find him. The father said in his word, if you take care of my kingdom, I will take care of you. Sometimes it is hard to give our money in church. If not for God we would not have any money in the first place. Everything on this earth is God after all. We have been in the church age long enough. It is time for us to be kingdom citizens now. The father says how long must I feed you milk. It is time for us to grow up and eat meat now. I have placed all my children on this earth to speak into someone life. But some of my children are lazy and they only think about their selves. What will I eat, where will I live, I do not have this and that. The father says stop complaining everything you need is on the inside of you. We must learn to tap into the spirit realm.

In the next couple of years it is going to get bad. People will be doing everything. You must be prepared to go to war in the spirit. There will be a lot of churches crumbling. There will be a lot of false prophets. A lot of my people are trying to water down the word to make it appealing to saints. My word must be like fire, which will convict them to live right. Please do not compromise my word pastors. A lot of big churches will fall by the way. My people are so hungry for the word. Please feed my sheep. I will find others to deliver my word if you cannot. I will get people in the street, prostitutes, drug addicts, whoever I choose to use. The saints that sit in the back will be thrush forward in this season. My people that you have look over and have not given a position in the church. I am not pleased with you. I will raise them up to go forth. Ministers of the word that are full of pride, you will be shut down. I have told you all before, do not touch my anointed, and you have put your hands on them. I hear them crying at night about the things you have done to them. You are very greedy! You are not content! These clicks in the church must stop. You and your family cannot run the whole show. This is GOD house. I am tired of the agendas that you have put into place. I want all my gifts display in the father house. If my children operate in the prophetic let them give a word. The word is coming from me. There are singers I have heard singing at night in their room because you want let them sing in your poor pits. They have voices like angels, but you want let them sing. I am not looking at what they have on you are. I am looking at their hearts. I am gathering up all my sheep that have been hurt and that have been put back behind everyone else. I am raising them up to take over for me. Like I said before. Touch not my anointed! This will be your down fall. It will hurt me more than it will hurt you. But as a father, I have to humble you. I love you and you must see the error of your ways my child.

Most of the church stays stuck in the old religion state of mind. Just like a piece of bread that is stale. We sit in church and we are stale. We don't clap unless the preacher tells us to. We don't stand up and praise the Lord unless we are told to. What are we robots or aliens. The spirit is moving sometimes and the singing is so sweet. We just sit back like we are dead. The father is not pleased with this at all. Then you cry out late at night about your bills and your problems. Why should he listen to you at all? People of little faith. Just like a hard piece of candy you try to bite into. It is stiff! Just like you! God is asking his children to remove the mask. It is the season when the fakeness will not work anymore. Even you children can look at you and see the mask. How can you expect to bring your children to church, when they see how you are when you leave church. The same nasty person you were before. The same hell raiser, curser, and who knows what else.

THE MASK

It is time to change, if we say we love the Lord and not our neighbor, how can that be. You wonder why your churches are empty today. People are tired of the same fake message and water down soup. I had a chance to meet someone that finally took off the mask and I ran. It was scary! The real person came out. But if we take it off slowly and really listen to people maybe it would help. (GOD) said I am tired of my children being stomped on by pastors. I will allow you to play church for so long. Then it is over with. The next season we will be in war. I am with you always, do not fear my child, and only trust me. You do not have to run to convention after convention, just get on your knees and pray. If my people, who are called by my name, would turn from their evil ways, I will heal their Land. Says the Lord! The father is trying to tell us something. You can't keep on sinning and think, you will be blessed. I have given you plenty of time to repent. Now I will begin a new thing. I will use whoever I please.

One thing I know for sure is that our father did not give us the spirit of fear. That our father gives us a sound minds. God says I gave you a voice to speak. I am in you and you can do all things through Christ that strengthen you. Just speak what you want today and you will have it. Then when I went home I got my children together. One of my children said God please bless my mom bank account, I am hungry god. You know as a mother when your child says something like that. It just tears you up inside. So I went back to my room, set down at my computer. Then something told me to get up. My father said you can talk can't you. So I anointed my wallet. I spoke to it. Then I had faith to believe it was there. So I went to get it. When I got to the bank I pulled out my debit card, and put it into the ATM machine. Nothing came out at first, so I tried another credit card. It was my son card. I said Jesus first, and then put the credit card into the machine. I got a very good surprise; a twenty dollar bill came out. I drove to another bank to make sure this was real. So I put the credit card in the ATM machine again. Then twenty more came out. I decided to look at the balance on the slip. I just started to scream! Jesus! Jesus! Jesus! I pulled the automobile over to the side of the road and got out. I just started praising the lord right there on the spot. This has taught me a valuable lesson about things you desire in life. If you are living right, by the word and serving the Lord. All you have to do is just speak it into the atmosphere, and you will have it.

A new spirit is awaking inside of me. I went to my prophetic class last night. It was very interesting. We had to speak a word into someone. This is the first time I spoke a word into a person life right in front of me. But I did it! I ask the father to stir up my spirit and send me a word for his daughter that pertains to her life. He did just that. The word I gave her was right on time. I feel I am stepping out more and more into my calling. Then this lady ask me was I a preacher. The other women said no. So they lay hands on the young lady after I had spoken over her. She needed to be baptized and filled with the Holy Ghost. That was the word my father had given me. But I believe soon as he makes me over I will be laying hands on people. It is strange when you step outside of the world system. You can listen more to God system of things for your life. My body is in the world, but I am not a part of it. The loud noise, beeping cars, idle chit chat gossip about nothing. All the hell that you have been through has to leave. You are about to birth something out. It is going to be hard at first. It will hurt for hours at a time. But when it comes out you will be brand new. When you are serving God you are forced to make a decision. God is looking for you to choose. Either you believe or you don't.

It is hard when you have bad habits to change. You just have to keep praying. I thought that this cigarette habit was kicked . . . but it keeps trying to come back. The devil is a liar. I ask my father this time to pull it up from the roots. Plus I bind it! So far it has worked out ok. Just like things in your life. You are a sales person and nothing is happening yet. You want to just quit. But God says you asked for this carefree position. You did not want to punch a clock. Now since you are not getting paid yet. It is not the time to give up. GOD says I though you said this time I will see it through. GOD says you knew it was 100% commission when you asked for this position. I always provided for you haven't I. So just as I was about to throw in the towel my strength came back. It is so hard, but I am birthing out something new in my life. I must change, and I realize that now. Thank you! Father that was a good word! The next day I went to church. The sermon was good. I was in a rush to leave to go to my Interview. It seems as if all hell broke loose. I did not make the interview, because of the traffic. The old car decided to stop on me. I said to myself, maybe if I had of stayed at church, this would not have happened. You should never stop praising the Lord. To dash off to appointments. If you have the favor of god on your life it will work out anyway.

Just stay positive and learn how to control your thoughts. It will be hard at time, but you must cast out all things that are not of the father. While I was on my way to church, I called my mother. Her negatively mouth and what she spoke over my vehicle came to pass. I should have not let it affect me. But we have lots of relatives that are negative, we must let their words go in one ear and out the other. A word spoken from another person can get in your spirit. We must learn to guard our mouths. If you do not have anything good to say do not say anything at all.

The more I am pulling away from the world. The old nature keeps trying to get me to go back. The devil is a lair. I am a child of GOD! He chose me from my mother's womb. We do not choose our parents, God does. They are just the vessel GOD chooses to get us carried in. Some do not want to be mothers. You ask why my parent is so drunk or drug head! GOD Says but daughter or son! You are in that family to change them. I only chose you! You are special to me. It will be alright daughter or son. I am all you need. But my child always honors your mother and father while they are alive. I will be there for you always. So if your family is disfuctionable do not let that bother you. I have put you in that family to save their souls. What God has desired for me to do all my life is coming to past. I see it so plain now. I must not give up. I must keep fighting the good fight of faith, for my bloodline, my kids and their children later down the line. Just like I tell my children, I am too blessed to be stressed. I just let them know in this life you are going to be tossed and turned. But if you faint not, Jesus will bring you out. No matter what people say, no matter what you're so-called friends say. Everything you lost you will get back. For your trouble you will receive double. You will receive double fire and double anointing. This time no one will be able to put your fire out. I went to church the other night to bible study. It was great; I had a dream that I would be touching the people. It came to pass. I felt the Holy Ghost on me. The pastor asks the intercessors to touch everyone. Then I went to speaking in tongues as I touch them. It was beautiful. I believe I will be healing the people soon. The Lord leads and I will follow. Sometimes I have to pinch myself and say self is this happening to you are what! I remember years ago before I had my children. I was in a bad car accident. I saw my life pass before me. Thank goodness I made it. My purpose in life was being birthed out. It was all in GOD plan. I am living out his purpose for my life. All I have to say is thank you Jesus for the pain.

The stone that was place there, thank you father for not removing it. Father thank you for the anointing. Thank you for letting me know, I have the power to crush the stone with my words. This life that we are living has many good times and many bad times. Sometimes you will have to suffer. You may say, well I am living right, paying my titles and all. Then after you give money in church, you don't have anything left. It could be maybe you are not giving enough. This is the last time I will be broke. I cannot feed my family, unemployed. I am too blessed for this mess. So if I have to give all my money and trust God I will. I am tired of beating my head up against the wall. And all I am receiving is zeros. It is time for my abundance to come forth. I went to another class at church last night. The things that happened were amazing. You think that people from your past you have forgiven. Then you find out that you have not let that pain go yet. So while I was crying out in the spirit, I let the pain go. All the people from my past that were not forgiven, I forgave. I am letting go of everything, things I can't fix. Things I tried to fix. I'm just letting go and letting GOD. He will take care of it all. Now that is a good feeling. Now I can rest in his arms. For the first time in my life I feel at peace. I am proud of myself for maturing in the Lord. If my heavenly father did not change me, I don't know where I would be. Now I take time to smell the flowers, plant seeds in the ground, get my hands dirty, it feels good. All the struggles that are taking place in my life are making me stronger. I am speaking into my life. No matter what, it will come to pass. I am meeting different people in the lord that will push me into my next level.

I talked to my African brother a couple of days ago. It was good to hear from him. I see he has moved up in the church now. He is a minister now. He was officially ordained to be a pastor and I am proud of him. He did not know I was an intercessor either. He has his own ministry now. I remember when we both worked together; he was so full of the spirit. It was all over him. All he uses to talk about was the goodness of Jesus. I knew then his steps had been ordered by God. Sometimes it takes us a while to figure out what our calling is. I believe when you are younger you make up your mind quicker. You do not have a lot of baggage or people holding you back. You are eager to do the work of the Lord.

My heavenly father watches over me and my children what an awesome god we serve. He knew I would be his again. He told me it was time to leave the city I grew up in. He started preparing me for my ministry. My heavenly father told me everything you need is inside of you. It is all in your mouth, just use your gift. You will never be broke again my daughter.

I would start volunteering for all the gospel programs. I did not know why. I would pray more and more talking to him. God was downloading things in my spirit. I was beginning to have a strong hunger for the word. Just like a vampire that needs blood to survive. I needed to be fed with the word daily.

It was like a fix to me. If I did not have my word that day I was miserable. It was time for my purpose to be birthed. I did not understand at the time. But now I do. My eyes are open wide. I'm in the world, but not of this world. I have been called for a purpose and a reason. To affect the atmosphere to cause change in the everyday people I meet. To share my testimony with people that are hurting in this world.

Church was on fire Sunday. We had a visiting pastor that had come to our church from the other side of town. We did not realize all the mess we had in our life. The trash that has to be cleaned up from our past life.

I remember when I used to sing karaoke. I did not feel like I belonged. I keep saying there has to be something better than this. I had to lose everything in order to save my life. My old self was beginning to die out.

I would go to a lot of revival and run around the whole church. Time can go by so fast. We forget about the promise we made to god. Now I remember. I was never content on any job. That was not my purpose. When you live a purpose filled life everything is much easier. You are very happy.

You just glide into everything the father wants for you. I had to depend on my father for everything. The father watched over me for a whole year and half. Even when I had no idea how I was going to make it.

My license was suspended for a whole year. I decided that I had to drive to get around the city. The father covered me and I was alright, without my father grace and mercy, I don't know where I would be.

The first time in my life I had to go to the pantry for food. I was about to cry. I could not handle it. That's when I just sat there and begin to write. I keep looking at the people around me. I did not understand! Why me?

Why did I have to be in this place? I believe the father wanted me to see how the broken people really live. I was so proud, and it was scary at first. The people at the pantry were some of the most humble people I met.

They did not have much, but they were thankful for what they had. It made me take a long look at my life. The way it used to be.

The hardest part when I moved to Indy was living in bad neighborhoods. I was placed here to learn how to humble myself. Living in this neighborhood made us afraid to go outside when it got dark.

The thugs were taking over the neighborhood. We would hear Gun shots all times of the night. Police cars and helicopters over the apartment complex. First I thought we had moved to Iraq. It was just like being in a war zone.

There were churches all around us. But the crimes keep happening day and night. The young teens would not go to school. They were content on breaking into people houses.

If that was not enough. Next they would break into people cars steal license plates and decals stickers.

One night it got so bad, they broke out the window downstairs. Starting shooting upstairs, looking for drug dealers. The police came, starting knocking on doors. I told the children to hit the floor.

The police allowed us to get out safely. Then I got mad! My Children said mom is it safe to wake up! Then I told the kids I would start looking for another apartment.

We prayed hard day and night for god to help me find a decent neighborhood to live in. When I went to sleep, I woke up with the vision of our new place.

A couple of weeks later we moved. I did not have all the money at the time. But god touches the landlord's heart. He waved the security deposit. The landlord let me moved in with a total of 250. The grace of God!

We started attending church in the mall. It was a nice place to be. The pastor really put on a show. I was beginning to feel the Holy Ghost more and more. My children loved the fellowship we had with other believers.

They would give out free doughnuts and coffee and juice every Sunday. The only thing I noticed was there were more street people than saints. But that was ok.

The pastor was trying to help them. He wanted to save their souls. He would pray over the people. We would sing songs on the video screen. We just had good fellowship.

The next Sunday the pastor told us. One of his trusted saints stole the collection plate. He told us who he was and asked for our forgiveness. I was surprised this happened. But sometimes you can't trust people when they are walking in the flesh.

We decided as the body of Christ to forgive him. The next Sunday, the guy who stole the money walks down front to apologize. I just told my children we would pray for him. Then a couple of Sundays later we did not see the guy anymore. I guess he felt bad and quit church.

Then next Sunday the pastor got up on stage and fell out. My children would just laugh. I told the kids he's a big man. I hope he is not playing with god. He has a good sprit he would tell everyone about their life.

I just could not understand the show. But the service was good. I just told the children each of us has to answer to the lord. I played in Church when I was 16. To me playing time is over.

But some of us have to put on a show to draw a crowd. Then when the Pastor told us he has to take the bible everywhere with him.

Even in the toilet, because he was afraid a spirit would come after him. I just shook my head. My children just laughed. God does not give us the spirit of fear. But I guess he was afraid.

We continue going to this church for a minute. I was beginning to get healed from my past hurts there. The pastor told me about my life. The person who had hurt me and I had not forgiven him.

I just started shouting! He was right on target. But you never know. So while I was at that church it was a learning process. I did not know it at the time. But god was healing me.

I was slowly forgetting about the past. I was coming into the light. The pain was going away. I was letting my father take control of my life. I did not listen to any worldly music.

It was best to just let go. It will be alright. The next day I went jogging. I met a nice man. He seemed to be a godly man. He would talk about god often. His name was James. At first he seemed ok.

He would pick me and the children up. He would take us to a house for Bible study group. He was such a gentleman. He would take us out to dinner.

I remember him always telling me to read the word to my boys. And make them read it too. I didn't know why at the time. But I do now. He was trying to move in on me. He would leave jogging suits over in the closet. He said it was for when we go jogging. Red flag No 1!

Then one day after bible study he seems different. He would talk about people in my neighborhood all the time. Women he saw on the streets he would call them names. I said brother is that nice to call people names. He said it does not matter they are prostitutes anyway. I began to question his motives. His nasty mouth made him ugly! How can a man say he loves God and have such a filthy mouth. He was a beast in sheep clothes. He was always praising the Lord in his car. He was always talking about what he did in church. He told me he was a deacon and sang in the choir. But if people knew the real deal they would run.

Then one day the icing came off the cake. He keeps calling me all day. He was cussing and hollering. I asked him what was wrong with him. I have not done anything to you. What is the matter with you.

He just hung up! Then he called back late that night. He keeps using vague language. I will not even describe it. I told him don't call again. He kelp calling for a couple of days. I keep telling him the same thing. Then he finally stopped calling. Finally he got the message.

If that was a godly man! I don't need to meet any more like him. He was a devil with sheep clothes on. I was glad to be rid of that nut. I guess I can honestly say, there were lots of red flags. I just chose not to believe them.

He seems like a man of god. At first I though he was a little mixed up in the mind. Maybe he will change. He changes alright! For the worse!

From time to time I feel like I'm being birthed out again. It feels like when I first got born again, at 25. I was up in Washington D.C. The spirit hit me and I was still fighting it all the way down to the front of the church.

I would look at the people knock out on the floor. Then I would say to my father. Ok I'm down here, but I'm not going to act like them! Trying to understand why I ran down the front. So they started speaking in my ear. Lying hands on me. They told me to speak! I felt it coming up in my belly. I just did not let it out!

But after church I told my pastor friend to pull over. He let me out at a park. I ran about 2 or 3 miles. The spirit was all over me. You could say I am a runner.

My heavenly father had to suffer. So do not think you can go through this life not suffering. He was a fighter and so am I. I am what he says I am. I can do what he says I can do!

It seems like sometimes you have to be moved out of your comfort zone. Then after you are out of it, the father can use you. You have no one to depend on but him. That is the way the father likes it.

We started attending this other church. It was very cool at first. But just like all churches they had their clicks in it. If you missed a couple of Sundays. They had this busy body person that would tell you about it.

They had a lot of fake people trying to sing with no anointing at all. Many are called to sing. But few are anointed to sing like angels. The kids and I were slain in the spirit. When we started going there they would look at us funny cause we were praising the lord.

I thought that's what you came to church for. Why waste your time and the pastor time. If you just wanted to be quite just stay at home. Next Sunday they had an evangelist come to the church to speak. I walked up front. She spoke in my ear. The dormant spirit that lay in me over 25 years came out. The Holy Ghost in tongues was so loud coming up out of my belly.

It was beautiful. I used to always run around the church and cry. But never spoke! It all came out. It had to take for me to move from my hometown to another city for this to happen.

The spirit that had been dormant in me came alive. It caught on fire! The anointing was all over me; I could speak in tongues as the spirit gave me.

I did not know I had so many gifts from the father. He gave me the gift to write his words. The gift of a seer in the spirit. But the higher the anointing the more you have to suffer.

God was beginning to stretch me. So every other service I would speak in tongues, and do pray for others. I don't know why but praying for others felt good. The father was making me over. The things I used to do I did not want to do them anymore.

The people I used to hang with I did not want to be around anymore. It was like I was being pushed into another realm. But I still did not understand my purpose. It was reviled to me a couple of years later.

My children are so smart; they told me there purpose in life. I told them that was great! Sometimes it take adults all of their life before they know there purpose in life. Then some of us die never knowing our purpose.

We choose the left road instead of the right road in life. Some of us just live for today. We do not think about no one but ourselves. It is all about me. I live for me and I die for me. How can I please me today? To hell with the children god gave us.

Some of us as adult waste our time doing the same thing over and over. We did not have any mentors growing up. We have to pat our own self on the back.

That's why it was so hard for people to decide what they want to be. No one was there to encourage us to go after our passion in life. So all we knew was to work hard every day and you will get a pay check. What a joke!

That's why there are so many dreams that are dead in the grave yard! Some people die with their dreams on the inside of them. But not me! I want my lord to say well done faithful servant.

As we turn the pages on another day. I feel like I am being tested. As I continue on the path of righteous, my life will never be the same. At times it feels as if you are losing everything. But the small things are nothing compare to the glory God will give you and then some.

Whatever you desire in life. Seek the father first and he will fill your cup over. Then after a while the world and everything in it is like a blackout. You see people of the world and you interact with them. But you have stepped into another realm.

No one can touch you there, no one can hurt you there, and all pain is gone. You have no past. You are like a floating spirit, watching the people on earth.

You're speaking in the spirit for them to get their life together. But no one can here you! It will soon be over with. But they keep on doing the same things as the children of Israel. Then you realize what the father has to listen to.

Thank God he has mercy on us, are else we can forget it. He could shut this earthly world down anytime he wants. But God is love, that's why he gives us plenty of chances to get it right.

We wonder why we have to suffer so much. Because we are hardheaded! He has to let us suffer to wake us up. God is love! He loves all his children. What is a father? If he does not discipline his children.

We make the father many promises. We know we do not plan on keeping them. But he forgives us over and over again. Our own earthly father would not do that. Most of the time we don't hear for him at all.

He was just a seed that god used to get together with our mother to produce us. That all he ever was. I do not even remember having a relationship with my natural father.

Sometimes in order to achieve more, you have to push yourself out of your comfort zone. If you want to be a millionaire you have to act like one. Study the way the successful people act. I was listening to the radio today. We are going to have a motivational speaker in town.

That is great! I guess I will try to make it. Then my mind said 25.00 can I afford it? I told my mind to shut up, I am going to get knowledge and it is priceless!

I see this so called recession is really a blessing. It is time for all the unemployed people to go into their own business. To not try to find work but to open up our own business.

There are all kind of grants and loans to help us get started. The father wants us to come out of the world system. Cross over into the spirit system. It is there we have dominion. We are rulers of our government.

It is just a small cycle that we are in now. It is time for us to jump in feet first while we can. Because at the end of the year it will be over. So we better buy them houses, start that business.

It is time for the last to be first for a change. If you missed the window period. You have no one to blame but yourself. As long as we stay in the world system you will be poor. That's the way the enemy likes it.

We must cross over into the spiritual kingdom. Were we have ruler ship and dominion? As long as we stay in the world system we will always be broke.

You have to go down, in order for you to come up. So no matter what you are going through right now. It is only temporary! It will not last my daughter or son.

So hold that head up high. Pull your shoulders back, and just walk in it. Like the queen or king I said you are. Be strong in the battle. Remember the battle has already been won.

God is tired of the greedy people getting ahead. They are being crushed in their greed. The window period is opening for us to step out of our box. I see more and more people on the street corners. They are holding up signs begging for money.

They need to use their mind or resources they have. While you are wasting time standing around on the corner. Get your hustle on! See what you are good at. You probably are good at working on cars, fixing hair creating items to sell.

Use your head and you will succeed! We have been laying back to long Waiting on a system to take care of us. It's time to dust ourselves off. Run with is no matter what. Just say, I can, I can, I can, I will, I will, I will.

Please stop the insanity. It is time to jump off the roller coaster. It is time to be who god created you to be. God helps those you help themselves. Start going back to church. It does not matter where you have clothes are not.

There are plenty of odd jobs around the church grounds. Let the people pray for you. Do not be afraid or ashamed we love you just the way you are. If you try to help yourself. The father will reach out to you and pull you in the fold.

A lot of people stay away from the church because of the hypocrites. Everyone wants a title. There are so many fakers in church. But you have to over look them. It is your soul that is at stake. God will deal with them.

I believe I saw my future husband in church today. He is a pastor and I will be his wife. Jesus is so awesome. When you think you have it figured out. He says! No daughter! I have it all planned for you. When you were in your mother womb. I formed you, for such a time as this.

When you are in church the married people are put before the singles. Why is that? I know it says he who fined a wife is a good thing. But being single, he who can endure singleness is a blessing in disguise.

Sometimes I feel as if someone or something has invaded my body. I know what it is, and it is beautiful. I am learning more and more about the kingdom system. Once you know how it works! It is awesome!

You will no longer cry all the time about your bills. Worry will be a thing of the past. Sickness will be gone! You may even get the chance to intervene for others.

Once you become a kingdom citizen. You are in charge! No more a Wimp! You do the kicking around things. You are in charge! No longer a slave to your circumstance. You have dominion! You have arrived.

There are seven gifts of the spirit. Jesus gives them to his chosen vessels. You may not receive all of them. But you will get one or two maybe three.

I am sitting here on my couch. I do not see this place. I see my house! I know it will come to pass. I don't know how I learned to decree and declare a thing. But I do it! My father must have downloaded it into my spirit.

I will be looking out my bedroom window! It will have a sliding glass door. With patio! Thank you Jesus!

It is strange, but what I normally do. I do different now! If I want to be somewhere else. I see it in my mind first. Then I am there! I had no idea that this is faith. But it is?

Sometimes I feel as if I have been forsaken. But I have not! Everything in hell is coming against me now. But I know why now! I'm beginning to Birth something in the spirit realm. No matter how I feel, I will keep on praying. I know it is coming through! God will work it out.

Picking up the pen tonight. It is the hardest thing to do. But I must tell my story. If I feel defeated I will be. If I feel woe is me, it will be. If I feel gloom, it will be!

But the devil, pick the wrong sister this time. One thing I have been all my life is a fighter. I will step all over the enemy head! I have authority! The father is in me and I am in him. As he said in his word greater is he that is in me than he that is in the world.

I can do greater works! I am the head not the tail! I still have so called friends trying to push me in their mess. I am too blessed to be stressed! I will not go backwards, but move ahead no matter what!

Sometimes the little voice in my head says, oh just give up. It will be much easier, go back home! But I say the devil is a liar! I will stand my ground and fight. You know you have to hear all these guilt trips!

Next week I am going on a three day fast. I'm going to do something. It will shock the hell out of my circumstance. Then next a 7 day fast. I'm glad I have some sister saints. They uplift me now! I will see them on monday night. I'm sleepy its 11:50 in the morning now. Good night now.

I just came from praise and worship service this Tuesday. It was kind of strange. We have new people moving up into positions all the time. I could not stop laughing. This lady got up and said she went into the night club to try to get people to come too church. She ended up drinking with some friends. It seems like no one has really changed their lifestyle. I pray that the pastor will get the spirit of discernment. Then he will see that every one that screams and hollers is not walking right. Until that happens we will see the same circle of clowns. So when I need a good laugh I go over to this church. If you want a deeper understanding of the father you have to read his word. Then it will be revealed in your life. It will show up in you. The spirit will convict you to live right. The way that you use to live, you can't live anymore. Oh you can easily fool the people of the church. Sometimes the church is just like the club. People cannot tell the difference now days. You cannot fool God. He knows all and see your heart. Every place the father sends you it is for a short time. He has to mature you. So where I am at now is the place that my father wants me to be. His anointing is all over me. He moves in me and through me. He helps me to bless other people. The heavenly father is changing me all the time. I am praying for everyone in this city. The Lord has already answered my prayers. I don't care what the world thinks or what my family thinks no one else matters. It can be a lonely road, but I must push on to get what the father has for me. In the end I will have my prize.

The kingdom works totally different then the world system. In order to get things moved In the kingdom we must have faith. It we have faith then we don't mind paying our tithes, when we come to church. The father gave you this money, after all. When we don't give as God has given to us. The devourer will come and eat the money up. This is what happens when we do not plant seeds to grow. In the Kingdom there will be a new system.

There will be no more stabbing each other in the back. There will be no more the rich keeps getting richer. It is about to be a change. My father is tired of this world the way it is. Now the tables will be turned, the scripts will be flipped over. We need to summit our will to the father's, after all he is the manufacturer of our life. All we have to do is read his word to fulfill our dreams he has for us. If you feel like you have lived here before you have. We were spiritual being before we became earthly. We have been here before as another person. Do you ever say to yourself? I believe I've been there before. Or that I did that before. Well guess what, you have! God wants us to dominate territories for him. He made us to be Kings and Queens. We are the head and not the tail. So me and my sister are going to begin to take some territory back. We will be starting on the east side of town. God said we could have all the land that we walk on. We are going to get the people out of the cage they have placed on their mind. They think that because I do not have anything I cannot do anything. We are going to start working with their mind. We will start are street evangelism to save the lost souls. We have to set the captives free. Once we free their mind they can begin to think for their selves.

CHURCH FOLK

Today me and the children went to visit another church. All the actors were getting ready to put on a play. When a certain person touches a button, they began to praise, or sing. Then when the musician hits a certain note it is time for the show to go on. I did everything I could to keep my children from laughing. They said mom what kind of place is this. I just told them everybody needs love, this is their way of getting it. When you get the word in you and you are filled with the Holy Ghost. You can see through all these actors. God told me to just be still, he will reveal the circus to me. He did just that and I did not like what I saw. So I am going to keep getting the word down inside of me. Let my father lead me where he wants me to be. I'm tired of being around baby saints that refuse to grow up. Get the word put it inside of you, eat it and you will change. But some of us are lazy, we have to be feed like a baby. If you don't read the word for yourself the pastors can't tell you anything. Some of the ways to keep the churches crowed is to let everyone in. Do not tell them about their sins, just take their money and say you will be just fine. You can do anything you want in this church; walk during service, your kids can climb under chairs. We have no order so it does not matter. Then we have the lay leaders 10 to 12 people trying to lay hands on someone. Most of these people need someone to lay hands on them. Everyone is trying to out shine the next person, just crazy. Next week I will take my camera to take pictures. But I must pray for these lost sheep. We all need to fill loved and appreciate.

THE BLOODLINE

Like my father said (Hosea 4:6) My people perish and are destroyed because they have no knowledge. You must know and live in the power to be a child of God. There are many blessing through Abraham that Jesus has left his children. Some of the things we have in us come from our bloodline. I did pick up one of my dad bad habits. I just asked the Lord to take it away from me and he did just that. You have faith that the heavenly father can do it. Faith can move mountains. Just give it to god and let him purify the bloodline. Sometimes we have people in our family that have very bad habits. You wonder why I can't seem to get rid of this spirit. Because it is in the bloodline, generational curse, it must be removed in order for you to function in the Kingdom. I asked GOD to take all that stuff out of me, purify my tongue, my mouth, and let me please him. When you began to walk in kingdom authority you can bind all generational curses in the bloodline. That's when I began to get more word in me I began ordering my day. I like doing this, it's like ordering your favorite meal. If you don't order your day it will be done for you anyway, by your enemy. So I asked the Lord to let the words from my mouth be sweet as honey. Just finish the work he had begun in me. I did not care about the pain I was going through. I just wanted my father to crush me, and that is what he did. After you go through you come out brand new. The old things you use to do, you do not desire to do them anymore. It is something about the Holy Ghost down on the inside of you. If you try to go back, it will convict you.

I went to bible study last night and it was great. My pastor talks about the hypocrites in church. He said we are always complaining about, the chairs, the carpets, the speaker of the house and etc. All of this is true. He said when we are talking about others we can't see our own faults. We are not perfect, only GOD is. I am glad that the father pulls out all the mess in us. The father has to clean up all the ugly parts in you before he can use you. The father said (Joshua 1-3) every place that thy foot shall walk on, I will give to you. This was the message tonight at bible study. It you read the word and study it and do my will children. I will give you whatever you need to make it in this life. The father gives each child what he wants them to have. I have met many Christians that have lots of spiritual gifts. But most of them are not living right. How can you call the father, Lord, Lord, and still live like a dog. We wonder why we are tormented and heavy burden. If the father uses you, just get ready for the battle. Just remember the battle is not yours, but it is the Lord. We just have to be strong and pray even when we don't feel like it. Even when we can't see how we are going to make it from one week to the next. Just pray and have faith, he will see you through. I have been letting this cold affect me today. But the devil is a liar. By his strips I am healed. I will praise the Lord no matter what the circumstance. Even if it hurts, it want stop my praise. A friend name Sharon told me in bible study that she had just lost her house. I told her I was sorry to hear that. She said oh don't feel sorry for me. I have given it all to the Lord; he'll work it out for me. She still had a smile on her face, and she was still praising.

Be careful of the tricks that the enemy uses. He will try to test you over and over again. He will use your friends, family, or co-workers if he can. He will start by bringing up things you like to do in your past life, before you got saved. He will try to take your mind off the word. Because if he can take your mind off the word, keep you from praising the Lord. Then he has you! So I read my word daily and meditate on it. It is like my weapon I use in my time of war. Without my word I would be lost. It is time now that we wake up, from our nap. The moving and the shaking is taking place now. It is time to invest in ourselves. It is now are never. Everything in this world is beginning to collapse, the stock market has already dropped, or bottom out. The business are folding up, and closing. Many people have lost their jobs. Some of the riches people in the world are going to prisons. There are many earth quakes happening now. The rich people in the world have abused people trust. My father is not happy with the state of the United States. My father says, if my people who are called by my name would get on their face and pray, I will heal the land. The problem is we have gotten too lazy to pray. We want everyone else to pray for us, hold our hands. If we could turn off the TV and other devices, and stop letting the media control our minds. We will not be influenced by all that trash that is out there. Then are minds would have time to concentrate, on what we are here on this planet for. We are not here to just take up space. God has made all of us for a reason, we have many problems to solve. Just think if we could solve the problem the father put us here to solve, we would not have to work for someone else. We would have plenty of money, less stress, less worry. To have a kingdom mindset is awesome. Every door you open, you can unlock it. When you are the King of your own territory, you do not have to punch a time clock. Now that is a great feeling all by itself.

The Lord said if I am about to build you up. I have to put you around some crazy folks. You have to stop looking at where you are at, but where you are going too. Without your haters and the enemy, you will not be processed. We must all strive to have a praise that will defeat the enemy. Your praise will bring you anything you need. I have always been the type that likes to come from behind. Just when you think you got me figured out. I have a lot of surprises in store for you. I will fight until the end. My father is trying to tell us this depression that the world is in is for our benefit. It is time for the children of Israel to take our land back. It is time for us to build our own cities and educational system. This is our time to prosper. There is a short window open now. We must jump in while the world is in travail. For all the dreamers it is time to take your place now. Just think of all the things that you never get done. You are two busy letting the media control your mind. We need to shut down all electronics systems we use on day to day basics. Just get some quite time in and just think. It will become clearer to you, what you were put on this earth to complete. We are all hearing for an assignment. If you do not find out what your assignment is you will be miserable. Your years will be wasted for nothing. You will die with your dreams inside of you. That is why change must happen. To make you step out of your comfort zone. To make you take action. What you create will save the next generation. Remember they are watching you. They are looking up to you. What do you want to be remembered for a zero or a hero?

I believe when we are trying to figure out things in are life it is hard. We must get quite and call on the Lord to help us. When you talk to God, tell him everything that has been affecting you. If you want to know what you are called to do just ask God. Man does not know your calling, only God does. You have to be willing to quite your spirit to listen for the answer. Sometimes when we go through a religionist system you see everyone being promoted in the kingdom except you. You say what is going on! It makes you question did God call you are what. God moves in due time, when he gets ready. If he has called you, then he has anointed you and appointed you. But he will let everything open up for you when it is time. So do not worry, if the church folk do not put you in your appointed place yet. God has something bigger and greater in store for you. You will rule a kingdom. You have been set aside for a time as this. You do not fit in the church clicks. The church is within you. My daughter or son I have called you, not the world. You will operate in my spiritual system. When the world system comes crashing down on their head. You will still be prosperous, in everything I have given you. So my daughter all I want you to do now is to sit back and watch as their system comes tumbling down. Church as we know it is just a building. I place my holy spirit inside of you my child. We have a lot of greed going on now in some of the poor pits. There are people doing everything and trying to put my name on it. I will not be mocked. There will be great famine in the land. There will be many earth quakes in the land. There will be great punishment for your sins my children.

This society as we know it wants everything to be instant. This is a microwave society! We have microwave ministers, that tell you to turn around three times and you will have your healing. Turn around three times and you will have a financial miracle. Sometimes you have to be slowed cooked first. You have to learn how to endure. If will not happen overnight. If things do not come to you in an instant, you do not know how to wait. The Moses generation, and the baby boomers are very hard headed people. They are stuck in their ways. But (God says) my children I am raising up will deliver my word with fire. I have waited for you to just step out in your rightful position. But you told me you needed this and that to make it. You used money as an excuse, or education as an excuse. I will take this new generation of babies from 3 years old and up and they will deliver the word. You wonder why the children of today are so smart. They are talking at an early age. They are on computers by the time they are 3. My army is being built to run things for me. You all have had your chance, now it is time for my young children to do the work. There will be 4 and 5 year old preachers speaking the word. I will call them from all parts of the world. Because you disrespected your world leader, another one will be raised up. I am rising up another leader that will take over the land. Right now he is 10 years old. He and his classmates will set laws in order. I want all my children to go back to the beginning and read my word. Please get an understanding, so you will not be a follower all your life. My people perish because of lack of knowledge. You are free now my people try to live free. It seems like the baby boomers are disappearing one by one. The earth is making room for the new generation. I hear some people taking like I don't know what to do with my life. Well if you don't! It will be decided for you. We have to get off of our own agenda and do what god has put us here for.

If saints could mind their own business in church everything would be alright. But we have old and young busy body trying to do the pastor job. Some churches are so clicks, you have to be quite. These people are dead anyway, why brother going. My heavenly father will fight my battle. I will just stand back and watch them fall. I see why they say the righteous walk is lonely. Most of the so called saints are mean, nasty, and back stabbers. If a lot of us did not turn the other cheek. We probably would be cracking some heads, starting from the top on down. You know that when you where in the streets you had to fight. But guess what! In some churches it is the same way. My father says child just be still, I will take care of these people for you. It may not happen right away. (God) says child I am always on time. There is no hurt in the world like church hurt. A friend told me this church hurt her. I said girl you have to forgive, forget, and move on. Do not let these busy bodies steal you blessing. There are greedy pastors and members that have their own agenda in the body of Christ. Then there are the pastors girls, they are in a click all by their selves. They are all competing with one another for attention. Then there are some pastors that don't really know anything their selves. They like to clown, and crack jokes, and talk about people in the poor pits. They do not have a sermon, so they just clown for an hour and half. Some of these preachers love the baby saints that don't know anything. They can tell you whatever. You have to be able to think for yourself. (God) says please my child read the word for you.

This one sister told me this one pastor told her that everything in the bible is not true. I said girl, you need to ask him what bible he is reading. But the father sees all. One day they will have to give an account for all their sins. A bragging spirit will be cut down. This one pastor said, I got my radio people and my church people. The radio people just call in for someone to cry with them. I have to treat them a certain way. I said oh is that so. Some radio pastors manipulate and pry on people feelings. Please stop sending in money to these false teachers. They are laughing all the way to the bank, at your expense. (God) will not be mocked! Whatever you sow you will also reap. It is like when you are anointed, no one wants to give you any type of position in church. I guess some of the pastors are afraid you will take over their ministry. We are all part of the body. I do not know why some pastors, are so insecure. I guess, I will pray for them. If you are called, you are supposed to teach and raise up the body. That is what's wrong with some of the leaders in the poor pit. They have too much pride, and are two arrogant. How can you follow a proud and arrogant leader? He wants to run the whole show. I believe that is what he is running a show. We know that shows do not last forever. So I will just sit back and watch his whole show crumple to the ground. This type of leader does not need to put oil on members and sinners in the church. He needs to pour the whole bottle on himself. First get the pride out of yourself, before you touch someone else. Just an example of another false leader!

This has been the hardest year of my life. But where would I be without my father. He has supplied all my needs. When I didn't have a job, he made the employer have favor on me. This is the God, I serve, he is just great. When I did not know how I was going to pay my bills. My heavenly father said daughter, I got your back. When there was not food on the table. He provided it for me and my children. Some days the car would not start and I would just call Jesus. Then after a while he would send me help. While I am writing this paper the tears are running down my face. I have to hide in the bathroom, so my kids do not see me crying. I have to stay strong for them. I have to remember every test and every trail is a revelation. God can mend my brokenness. Sometimes I get depressed and the old flesh says, hey just smoke a cigarette. But the God in me says no more. You are just going to stand this time around. It is your time now. This is just another battle with the flesh, and the spirit has won. We will have a lot of times when we are tempted to go back to our old ways. Just because you are saved and filled with the Holy Ghost. There still will be lots of times when you are tempted. We must continue to pray, and fast, so our father can slay the old man for good. I hear this preacher get up in front of the church and say he just got his old nature under control a year ago. I said oh! I did not know some ministers still struggle with their sins. That just goes to show you some sins are harder to get rid of. But I believe if he had of summited to the father first before he start preaching the word. Then it would not have been so hard for him. Then he is up in front of the church telling people to let him lay hands on them. I just said to myself, the devil is a liar. I feel sorry for the wife, when these so called pastors tell their dirty laundry in front of everyone. That is one reason why the sinners in the streets do not want to come into the church.

To become a citizen of the kingdom, you are summiting to God will. You are saying Father, I trust you with everything I have, my heart, mind, and soul. When you are walking in the will of God. Things become much easier for you. Your life will prosper in the middle of recession. Everyone will be telling you girl, I am broke. You will just look at them an smile. If the king owns you and all the resources in the world are his. You must know he will always provide for his children. Now if you are not walking with God, you should not expect the father to take care of you. Just like your natural father, he only takes care of his children, not outsiders. This year things as we know it are getting ready to be shifted. We have been too lazy and not doing what the father has called us to do. That is why the shifting is about to take place. We worship a king because we love him, and he owns everything. We have kingdom privileges when we worship the king. If you are not a kingdom citizen, you should not expect any benefits from the king. When you understand kingdom, you don't need no hymns to get you excited. You don't need a praise team to get you happy. You already have the hymns inside of you, and the praise is something you do every day. You wake up in the morning praising the Lord for another say. We as the body of Christ must not sit back and wait for someone to prompt us to move. We must not wait for things in our life to fall apart before we develop a relationship with the father. It's only going to get worse in this world today. Just like in Moses days, the children of Israel are hardheaded, stubborn people. This is your second chance. (God) said I came so that you can have life and have it more abundantly.

This is my year of Jubilee. The father is going to release some things to me. But first he has to release me from some people. The father has already sent the answers to my prayers. But sometimes unseen forces are holding it up. I am getting ready to get a break through. I am getting ready to break through in the spiritual realm. God is getting ready to shift me. He is shifting me into a different realm, more joy, more peace, more power, more anointing! My father is helping me to discover the strength that he put down on the inside of me. God wants us to know, we can live the life of our dreams. We must find people that are not afraid to speak the word into our situation. We must always have a covering over us. Everyone needs someone to keep them accountable. If not they will drop off the scene. We must get off are butts and stop being lazy. Please stop looking for jobs, the job is inside of you, God gave you everything inside of you to use. We just have to work are minds and stop depending on a system to take care of us. We have been brain washed long enough. God gave us skills that we have to tap into and use. Just like you like to do hair, sew clothes, work on cars, make things like jewelry. Well stop being afraid to use your skills to start your own business. If we want to change a system it has to start with us. Stop looking for the government to take care of you. They will take care of you alright. When you can't take the knife in your back anymore, you will begin to work your brain. Just like some of the pastors, that doesn't work. They use their brain to get you to take care of them and their family. We must use are brains to help pull ourselves up from the pit of poverty. No one is going to tell you this, so just listen to this word my people.

Just like an egg that has been in the shell all its life. At some point the egg gets crack open. It is time for us to come out of our shell and walk out the purpose God gave us. We all need to use are gifts are they will dry up. Please do not take your gift to the grave, because of your laziness. Sometimes I think about some of my friends back home. I say thank you Jesus for pulling me out of the crowd. One thing I can say about God people, we are not beggars. The father gives us the ability to go get it ourselves. Sometimes we just have to pray until the door comes open. We have to just lie out on the floor before our father, and humble ourselves I believe when one door shuts, another one will open. God leads us by the spirit. You are the sons and daughters of God. You have not received the spirit of bondage again to fear. But you have received the spirit of adoption, whereby we cry, Abba, Father. The spirit itself beareth witness with our spirit that we are the children of God. When you speak over yourself and have faith it will come to pass. We are a speaking spirit; all we have to do is open up our mouths. We just have to order our day. Just like you decide what you want for breakfast, lunch, and dinner. I am speaking over myself right now, and I believe the things I just said will come to pass. No matter what I will push my way through. No matter how hard it is I will stand.

The heavenly father paid a price for me. Now it is time for me to be free indeed? Free from bad habits! Free from bondage! Free from sin! I just want to move like my father. I've carried weight around for too long. Now I choose to just let go. Just let go of the past, let it go! I am free at last! Thank God almighty I am free. Free to live my life by design. The design my father had intended for the beginning of my Life. I believe we all can live by design, if we just let go of the trash that is junking up are Bodies.

Sometimes we stay so busy doing nothing. We are so busy wasting time. If we would stop being so busy, we could complete what the father has put us here to do. Life is not that hard. We must follow the father principles for the kingdom living. He will bless us exceedingly and abundantly according to his riches and glory. The God in you will make you say yeas instead of no. To be transformed by the renewing of the mind. Then when you can see like the father, you get to look at all the ugly in the world. You don't ever want a part of it. You have finally arrived. You have crossed over to the spiritual realm. Have you ever tried taking your body where it does not want to go? We'll I've tried that many times. My body says you are strong you can do this and that. My mind says who are you kidding? So I have to shut out the thoughts in my mind, and that can be a process. I have to let the spirit guide my life. It may seem scary at first. But I must walk on. I will take a lot of bumps along the way. I must do what I love to do every day. I must live in the moment not yesterday. It is so easy to go back to the past. But when I think about all the mess, my father pulled me out of I will never go back again. My future looks brighter than my past, and it puts a smile of my face. Now that is worth fighting for. I believe once you learn how to control the billions of thoughts that flow through your mind on a daily basis. You will have accomplished a whole lot. Because whatever is controlling your mind. It is in control of you! You might want to try just replacing the negative with positive thoughts on a daily basis. Just cast it down at the root. As soon as that though comes to mind, try binding it in the name of Jesus. This will help clear some of the clutter in the mind.

PHONE CALL

Then my phone rings, hey Tonya what's up! Girl did you hear about Phil. Yes I heard! I believe it is God will to see a person gets the right position they need. But if you keep getting laid off, I believe he is trying to tell you something. If they keep shutting the door in your face. It is time to try something new. I told Phil just step out and create your own business. I told him to invest in his self. He told me he loves to cook? Girl I told him to just open up a restaurant or something. But girl I don't know what went wrong with Betty. It's like she has a screw loose in her head or something. She is not working either. But Betty problem is she keep applying for these dump jobs with crazy hours. She is so talented, I she all her gifts and I told her about them. I told Betty to stop busting her head up against the wall. These temps companies will just use you and then kick you to the curb. Don't be so desperate. Then I asked her who has taken care of you for two years. She said girl you know God has. Then she said I just need funding to get my products off the ground. Then I told her to just be creative. I told her if she would ask her heavenly father, he will help her. Like they say, he doesn't come when you want him, but he is always on time! Then she said you know Shirley, you are right. I am going to stop being afraid and just do it. My father did not give me the spirit of fear, but of a sound mind. So I believe, I can do it, thanks girl.

I believe if we can just keep praying when times gets hard, that will help. The enemy knows your destiny. You are more than a job. You have greatness inside of you. Just let it out, let your life shine. Someone is waiting on your gift! You have to serve the world with your fruit first, before you can be promoted. You will be happy, you are so close, I can taste it. You know all my life my mom always said, are you working, what job you doing now. That used to get on my last nerve. I guess in her generation that's all they know how to do. Forget about your dreams, just work, work, work, until you drop and die. One time I asked her mom, what kind of life is that? She just said that is what you are supposed to do. I said why is that. She did not have an answer for me. I told her, I feel there is more to life. You have to live, not just work a job, retire, and die. She just got quite. I know she probably though I was crazy. But I am just wired differently. It has taken me a long time to figure that out. Some dreamers are in the right position to fulfill their dreams. We are leaders! I know I have a calling on my life. I feel it every day. I can be riding in my car or ministering to someone, and the spirit takes over me. Sometimes we spend so much time in or cars, and at work. That we don't take the time to spend talking to the father. The father loves us; he just wants us to fellowship with him. It does not matter if you have done wrong, just ask for God forgiveness. You don't have to be perfect to come to the father. He will accept you as you are. The sinful nature of man makes us struggle. When God corrects us we take issues with that. Love for God will change you. If you really love me you will strive to keep my commandments. God brings us into awareness of our selves. Now you are more in tune to the things he does not like. For instance if you have a problem with stealing before. It will be more of a problem now. Everything you do, God will say stop. But sometimes we are hardheaded and do it anyway. It's like the spirit and flesh are fighting against one another. Now that you are a Christian your spirit has come to life.

The father said if you will take up my life and walk with me. If you can, try to give up everything, this world will offer you. Life will only give you pain, suffering and disease. (God) says I want to give you eternal life. You will not want for nothing my child. I will supply all your needs, just ask me. It seems like when you are going through in a strange land. You have no family, friends, only Jesus. It makes it easier to trust him. You have to call on your heavenly father for everything. That's the way he likes it. The father wants to take care of his children. You may say! It has been too years, and I'm still in this mess. But God does not move in our time zone. He is eternal and not on a clock, like we are. All the years, you have lost. The father will give them back to you, in due season. He will stop the aging process, just open up your mouth and ask. The father says I love you daughter or son. Do not just let me into your life on Sundays. I want to talk to you every day. Let me know what happens at work, and at school. (Jesus) says I need to know about the family and what happens to you on a daily basis. If you love me my child, trust me with the inner most secrets of your heart. I will not hurt you, I will just help you. When you hurt daughter or son, I hurt too. Now if you're earthly father will give to you. How much more do you think your heavenly father will take care of you? I did create the whole universe for my pleasure. My child at all times be yea sober, because, the adversary will try to temp you. My child ask me for strength, when you are week. I will give you the will to handle any situation. Just ask! Seek me early in the morning, before you begin your day. My child begin to order your day. Speak into the universe what you want to happen today. Then the universe will bring it to you. My child things will just happen to you, if you don't order it. You do not want your day to be ordered for you. It may not taste too good.

If you focus on your situation, it will make you scream. You look at your life and you say what a mess. What has happened to me? I had all this money at first. I was financial secured, years ago? Then you begin to wonder, did I take it all for granted. You begin to wonder about the times you were just blowing money. This was not a need in your life, you just wanted it. Then when you reach rock bottom, you come to your senses. You cannot get the years back, you threw away your funds. I believe when we summit to the father's will, he will replace everything that was lost. I love my heavenly father with all my heart. I am not looking for anything. I just want him to make me over again. The flesh is trying to control your mind. You just have to say flesh not this time. I am walking in the spirit. You have no more control over my thoughts. It will be hard at first, it is a daily walk. You become more sensitive to the father will for your life. Lord knows you have done it your way for long enough. You begin to see the results that did not happen your way. You think about all the gifts, God has given you. It is time to put these gifts to use. It is time to work smarter not harder. You find yourself not completing assignments. It can get you in a lot of trouble. You see others moving up to your post. Things you know that God has called you for. You start to run from all the church meeting.

Then you say did they forget about me. They did not forget about you? They just do not know how to read you. One minute you are here, the next minute you are at another church. (God) says please my daughter stop running, so I can use you. You have to sit still under leadership. You are a great saint, but I cannot use a rebel. Your ministry will start soon, if you learn to submit. (God) says these gifts I gave you are for the church, not yourself. I know you think you are all that and a bag of chips, but daughter you are not!

When it seems like everything is moving along great. Life throws you a curb ball. You forgot to ask God before you decided to move into a new place. When you go outside his will for your life, things happen. So I found this duplex and just moved in it. I said well this is great God has blessed me with a new home. God was not in this place, because I did not ask him first. I just saw the place, and decided to move in. We had not been in this place a week when all hell broke loose. This place was cold, and had pests in it. So I told my kids, we don't have to live like this. So we moved right out. I did not think about the next place. I just left; we could not sleep at night with all the critters in there. You never know how the homeless person feels until you are almost like them yourself. I tried to get another place after place, but my money was not right. So I pray so hard every night and cried myself to sleep. I said what kind of God lets me go through this. The children and I had to sleep on somebody else floor at night. It was cold and unpleasant! I did not understand what I had done wrong. I just remember a pastor telling me in this life there will be trails and tribulation. I also remember the father saying my anointed will go through many test. I am just maturing you for the kingdom. It does not mean, that I don't love you my child. At the time this was happening, I did not see this. So after I got through fussing with the father. I just figured he was not going to help. I had a plan b to use. You know everyone always has a plan b. The next day I dropped off the children at school. I just started singing, it was taking my mind off my problems. I did not have all the money to move. I had asked church after church, no one would help. So my plan b was just borrowing the money. I knew deep down in my heart, I did not want to do that, but I had no other choice. So I went to the storage place to put more items in there.

While I was there my phone rings. I said to myself who can this be, calling me this early. It was a lady from the apartments that had turned me down. She said is this miss so so. I said yes it is. She told me to come and get the apartment, it is mine. The lady said, do you have $250.00 on you. I said yes! The lady said, get a money order. When I hung up, I knew it was my father. No one else knew what I had in my pocket. I just started screaming and praising the Lord right in that storage unit. Sometimes I talk too much. So I guess, my father said, I had your back all the time. I was just waiting for you to shut up, and let me go to work on your behalf. He was saying I just needed to trust him. Now I really do believe what people say. That he may not come when you want him too, but he is right on time. All I can say is God is continuing to crucify the flesh. He is teaching me to put all my trust in him. Lean not to my own understanding. In everything I do, I will acknowledge him. My heavenly father is the author of my life. If we all would just give back, the knowledge that is shared with us. We could affect a generation. Then real change will take place. We are ignorant of our inheritance! If we knew how fast we could move in the spirit realm.

We could affect every city, and change would take place. We would run to the father, and say sign me up sir. The world system has us all confused. We must step out of the world system into the spirit system of doing things. This is when your life really begins. This is my father all over me now. I am taking the time to ask him. What is his will for my life? I am getting out all the clutter in my mind. I am finally free to just live the way God had planned at first.

Being reborn is new and exciting. All the old you is being crushed out. The flesh is steadily trying to fight the new spirit within you. The spirit says flesh man you have to die. The flesh says no? The spirit says it is my time to shine? It is true what they say! When the praises goes up, the blessing come down. You can take the wide road if you like. Keep doing drugs, drinking, men and womanizing, sex, outside of marriage. Then you are living in hell right now. Now if you are smart. I would take the straight and narrow flight. You can have peace right now! You will have eternal life in the future. Our father wants us to experience kingdom living right now. We don't have to wait until we die to live like kings. This land is ours for the taking. We just have to work our minds. Everything we need is already on the inside of us. We just have to pull it out. If you say daddy, I need help, he will help you. He wants us to be able to take territories for the kingdom. The father wants us to be able to train others in his army. We are in the fight of our life. The kingdom vs. world order. We have already won in the spirit realm. We must win in the earthly realm. Little David was afraid to beat goliath the giant. We must stop being afraid to beat the giants in our life. The struggle is over for you. (God) says I come that you might have power, and have it more abundantly. You have power to speak things in your life and say move. Get thee behind me. My child it takes power to live in this life. If you have no power, you get no keys. The more power you have, the more keys, I will give you. I will give you the keys to unlock all the doors. Right now my child these doors are a mystery to you. I just want to share myself with you. So when the world sees you they see me. You will have the keys to heal all the sick in your land. Sickness will be a thing of the past. My wisdom will make you rich.

Sometimes we can rush things and do our will and it does not work out right. The father says come to me all that are heavenly burden. I will give you rest. The seasons are beginning to change from fall to winter. This is when our life changes. The winter is the season of completeness. Whatever was started in you in the summer is already done in the winter. It is cold outside, and the words I have given you are in you. You just have to be still long enough for them to come out.

You say father I am lonely, where is my husband? The father says; serve me with all your heart and soul. Then my daughter, I will give you the desires of your heart. Then you ask the father for a new house or car. The father says everything you need, it's on the inside of you. Just speak and have faith that you already received it. It will come to pass my child.

The father is steadying moving and is everywhere. (God) says I am not a person, but I am a spirit. I can move so fast before you can blink your eye lid. I want all my children to fulfill their mission in life. There are enough people in the graveyard, with unfulfilled dreams. The next young educator is dead. He just got shot in the head. The lady that was going to build a 600 square feet recreation center for the youth just died. The first women owned car dealership just died. The guy that had a great idea of how to cure cancer, just died. He got run over last night. I don't know about you, but I am tired of lazy people dying with stuff inside of them. I look at the three and four year old children now. They are very smart and articulate. I believe by the time they are seven they will create products to market for themselves. I believe sometimes a couple of generations, gets skipped. If it looks like they are tired.

My heavenly father says, I will used who ever. The other day in church, this little seven year old was praising the lord so much. I asked this lady do you think he's faking. She said no girl, he's for real. Now all the old people were sitting down. This little baby was just praising his head off. I could easily say, he will be preaching by the time he turns ten years old. I believe the teenagers have been skipped. The father is going after the babies. They have a pure spirit, which has not been tampered with. They have not been brain washed by adults yet. The father wants us to be on fire for him. The babies are on fire. You cannot be hot one day and cold the next. Some preachers get tired of speaking the word. They play let's make a deal night. The father is not making no deals with his word. If you are tired and do not have nothing to talk about, please just sit down. Your replacement is just around the corner with a word in his or her mouth. I see the three and four year olds setting the next grid for the kingdom. The duplication process has begun! Now the shift is taking place today. We are being pulled out of our comfort zone. The things you use to do, are not fulfilling to you anymore. The father is pulling on your heart to get it right before you leave this world. There is a gut feeling deep down on the inside of you. The feeling is telling you, there is something else I need to be doing for God. I believe if you do not do it, you will be sick on the inside. I believe like never before, people are trying to find out their purpose in life. They may have waited a long time to find out? Some people wait until they are forty, or fifty, or sixty to find out. But never the less, God is pulling at their heart to get it right. They are looking at their grandkids and see the love and joy in their heart from the Lord. They are wondering where it came from. This joy came from the father himself. The father is teaching the babies.

Sometimes your flesh wants to run back to where it is safe at. But there is no safe place in the world. You know you have to step out of the box. You might as well start doing what God has called you to do. The number one thing that holds people back is fear. Fear of the unknown, fear of what people will say. Then sometimes that little voice inside our head says, girl you too old to do this and that, who you kidding. Then we have the fear of achieving all our dreams. I believe we need to just squash all those crazy ideas out of our mind. Just like you step out to take your first job, or to finish school, it takes effort. You will be what God has called you to be. If not you will live your life miserable. God is asking for his children to take a stand. It is time for the Godly army to stand up and fight. The enemy has been kicking you upside your head long enough. I would be tired of being stomped on. You learn how to fight in the flesh when you were a child. Now it is time to learn how to fight in the spirit realm. The spirit realm works differently than the flesh. You must open your mouth and decree and declare a thing. Then it takes a whole lot of faith to activate the word. I believe in order for the children of God, to walk into their kingdom authority. We must operate in the spirit realm. We cannot move anything with our flesh. You can cry like a baby about your problems and your life. It will not help your situation. You should be tired of the enemy stealing your homes, marriages, and your children's life. It is time for God army to form a revolution. It is time for us to live on top of the world. We are more than a conqueror, we have been redeemed. It is time for us let everything come out of us the lord has put into us. We must stop being hardheaded like the children of Moses.

It's time for us to pull out all stops. Each city we travel to, it is time to get God army together. We must take our children back from the grips of the enemy. No longer must we conform to children having babies. We must teach them the way of holiness. We must no longer let our children be slaves to a corrupt world order system. We must train their minds to fight in the spiritual realm, not the flesh world. We must be kingdom builders, spreading the word to all. This is our time to take back what we lost years ago. It is time for a Holy Ghost party! I believe it is time for the churches to step up to the plate and be accountable. No longer can we have dead churches were the people come to sleep. We need the churches to go out to the streets and get the people to come in. You have an ordained mission in life to save the lost souls. The people that are already in the church and the children, that are on the street corners. The church needs to be a hospital, taking in my sick and lost servants. How can you get up every morning putting on your Sunday's best? Then you ride past my lost child and do not pick him up, to take with you. You have seen them everywhere, on the street corners begging for food. You see them walking down the street, with their belonging on their back. You don't talk to them cause they smell or stink. These are my children too. Just as I love you! I love them also. If my churches would go out in the neighborhoods and get my children, all of God house would be filled. I do not want to hear you crying no more about why me Lord! Why not you? Go out and let your light shine, I gave you. Please stop asking me for anything. I have given you enough, and you have done nothing with it. I hear you crying at night my child. (God) says but do you understand the words that are coming from my mouth. No longer can you close your eyes when you see my children hurting. I blessed you so you can be a blessing to others.

We need to turn off the TV and radio and be about God business. It's time for us to put the father first in our life. You can't just pull the father out on Sundays, and then on Mondays go back to the way you use to be. You must put on all the armor of God every day of your life. We all should be sick and tired of doing the same things, and getting the same results. At some time in your life, you need to jump off the Ferris wheel. It is time to surrender to God's will for your life. It is time to walk in faith. People overseas have been taking care of themselves for the past couple of years. They stick together like thieves in the night. It is time for America to wake up. We must fight the good fight of faith. We need all of our soldiers back home to fight for the family. We have people starving in the United States. But yet we feed people all over the world. Something is wrong with this picture. We must take care of home first, before we can take care of the world. It is time for parents to step up to the plate and sit down with your child and learn them yourselves. Do not expect anyone to care about your baby. The truth of the matter is, they do not care about your child, whether they learn or not. The world order system is set up for your child to fail. That is why you must take the time and teach them yourself. We can no longer leave our children's mind and education to others. It is time to invest in our future, and leave the past in the past. (God) says I came that you might have life, and have it more abundantly. I just want my children to live like the queens and kings that they are.

It is so strange but everything that has happened to you has already been done in the spiritual realm. You just have to step into it. You are living out your future now, whether you like it or not. We create our own happiness in life. So if you are not happy with the outcome of your life, just change it. You get to create the way you want your life to play out my child. It is like we have this big screen in front of us each day. Instead of just letting the picture play for you. You can create a different outcome yourself. If there is something about the big screen play you don't like, well jump in and change it. Our God is an ever moving spirit. He does not stay in one place all the time. Now if we as his children have his spirit down on the inside of us. We can move into different channels just like our father. So why do we limit ourselves to being stuck in any situation. Now when you are watching TV. Do you sit and watch the same channel over and over again. If you did that, it would be insanity. So just like the TV channels you change every day! We must change the channels in our life. If we don't, we will become stuck in the same old patterns. I believe that if you cried every day for help, this will not help you. We must take action if, we want to change the outcome of our life. If you are in an apartment, and you say to yourself. I would love to be in an house someday. Then you do nothing about it. Well guess what, you will get nothing. If you feel you don't fit in the world system, get out of it. The kingdom system has been waiting for you all your life. Ever since the time you were born. God create you and put clothes on you. It is you that have turned your back on the father. We are all very creative, just like our father. The father has put his DNA, in you. So if we are creative like him, we must create. He did not put us here in the earth, to work a boring job. He sent us here to solve problems. If you can solve some problems in life, you will be rich.

We must use the passions and the gifts down on the inside of us. We will not want anything. How can you be a blessing to others, if you do not work your gift. The gifts God has put inside of you is not for you, but it is for others. You will fail all your life if you don't work your gifts. I tell my children every day, baby go after your dream. Don't wait until you get old and grey and try to start doing something. If you can just use what God gave you now, you and your family will be prosperous. That passion is your destiny. We must stop wasting our time. Time sits still for no one. One minute you are twenty, the next minute you look up and you are fifty. You say where did the time go. We live in an every changing universe that is steadily moving. It is so important to live your life as the Lord has birthed you to live, and then you will have no regrets when you get old. One thing for sure, we all will be going somewhere. I'd rather go to heaven, then hell. You must command your atmosphere to work for you. Every day we get up, we must take control over our life. Just like Lazarus got up, from the grave yard. We must get up! We must speak to those things in our life that tries to hinder us. (God) wants us to put on all his armor. So we can stand against the wiles of the enemy. We must put (God) first in our life. I believe it we want peace of mine. When you have peace the enemy cannot attack you. You know that God has your back. God has given us the spirit of love and a sound mind.

When we do things sometimes we create a chain reaction. This happened to me when I and the children were going inside a restaurant. I taught my children to hold the doors open for ladies. So when we were coming out of this restaurant this older lady, had walking issues. Her son was helping her into the restaurant. My son held the door for them. Then after we left and got into the car. I saw all the men customers holding the door open for the ladies. I said to my children, how great is this? We have created a chain reaction today. You send your vibes out into the universe for whatever you want. If we think love toward others, we will get love back. If you want a husband, just image yourself walking down the aisle. Now sit back and think, what color dress do I want to have on. Think about the way you want your future husband to look. Now place your order to the universe, and you will have what you speak. We can order good food to eat, so we should know how to place an order for a good husband for our lives. You must tell the father what you want, he cannot read your mind. We are speaking spirit, the father just wants us to talk to him. People in your life come and go. Sometimes they are there for only a couple of years. They are placed there for a reason that you do not know. No one knows the plan God has for your life. Do not hold on too tight to these people. We must grow through seasons, to help us achieve our greatness. Everyone cannot go through this journey with you. You must begin to shed off layers to be great. It will hurt, but when the butterfly in you comes out of the egg, it will be great. You are able to fly around the whole city. You are still living in the city. You have just crossed over into the spiritual realm. It's like heaven on earth, everything you though it would be. You wonder what has taken you so long to cross over. That stubborn will of yours. The father had to fix you. You were kicking and fighting all the way. Then you just decided enough is enough. My way is not working, I might as well trust God.

Today it is time to just wash it off. Wash off the pain of your past life, just wash it off. Today is a better day, today is the day the lord has made. You ought to be glad in it. While you are washing it off, just praise the lord. When you have been going through hell just wash it off. The father just wants us to be clean in the body, and in order for this to happen, we must just wash it off. My child before you can begin to minister to anyone, let my word minister to you. It is through this word, I will heal you, and all the broken places in your heart. Then after I have healed you I will send you forth like pure gold, one of my remnants. It is so hard sometimes to step out of the boat. When you step out you are looking around for your help, and there is no one there. It feels like you are all alone at first. Then you begin to remember what the father said. Your footsteps, my daughter are ordered by me. I will never leave you or forsake you. It seems when you are out of the boat, all hell breaks loose. Things you though you could count on, just get harder. There is no one to talk to about your problems. Then you remember the problem solver, is your father. It takes faith to be strong in the mist of the storm. Just know, my daughter you are not in this storm by yourself. I am with you! When you feel the wind blowing, that is me your father. When you are all chocked up, and do not know what to say. I have given you my holy spirit. Just pull on it, when you need me my daughter. Then you begin to take your eyes off your situation. You look at some people on street corners, sleeping that don't have a roof over their head. Then you say, father forgives me for complaining. I am very thankful, for what I have. Sometimes the hardest test in the world is placed in your life to mature you. We can no longer go around like babes, sucking on a bottle. The father wants us to grow up, so he can use us, for the kingdom.

Sometimes you find yourself sitting in church after church for years and years. Then the father says daughter or son it is time now. Just when you think the father has forgotten about you, he calls you. It is your season, to just walk it out. Now at first, you were ready to do everything in the church. But when you kelp getting pushed to the back, time and time again. You just said well forget it. What you did not know, is that it was not your time. When we move out and do things out of order. This does not please the father. This may please our flesh! But we must move when the Holy Spirit gives us orders from God. When the father orders are steps, he has everything worked out for you. You don't have to sweat anymore over the small things in life. Sometimes I believe when people don't have much they are more humble. I see this all the time. I just sit back and observe the way some church folks act. Then sometimes I just sit back and watch the pastors. I am so glad, I can see in the spirit. I can see right through them. So I just over look a lot of things. I am so glad my heavenly father is calming my spirit. I have lot's more patient than before. It is like a cake cooking in the oven. Now the cake is not done yet, but you try to take it out anyway. If you take the cake out of the oven early, it was fall. Now, that is just like you. If God send you out too early to deliver a word, or lay hands on the sick. You will not be quite ready. No matter how hard it is, the father has to finish processing you. He has given you a mighty anointing. With that comes power! He must finished processing you, so that you can heal others. It has been a long time since a local person healed the sick. You were created to do signs and miracles just like Jesus. So when you think, you can't take any more just call on Jesus! He is you rock!

The lord is saying what is driving you. The lord says in the end I will examine what you did. You know pride is so tricky, especially in the church. You are constantly in and out of this world. The warfare will be forever. It will take a minute for your flesh, to agree with what God said. You have to be careful, that your pride does not drive you out of the will of God. Do not let anything wrestle with your walk of God. Do not let your pride, take over your purpose. We must stop using the poor pit to bash people about their faults. Some pastors get up in front of the congregation and just make a joke out of their self. They have not studied the word the night before, so they say I will just wing it. I will start talking about all the single ladies and what they need to get a man. Then I will start on other things to chat about. First of all pastors, make sure your home is happy! Do not tell us what to do to get a man. I believe some of you are sleeping with half of the ladies in the church anyway. You may just want to put a zip on it. My father's said keep the sanctuary holy ground. So if you don't have anything holy to talk about just be quite. Now if you look around and there are only 12 people sitting in your place. You may need to adjust your weak message. It is past time that the message of God, go out with fire, not water, or milk. When I was a baby, there was plenty of milk. Now sense I am an adult, I need the meat of the word to fill me up. Saints are moving around from church to church, looking for meat. Just maybe if your word was not so weak, they would stay. It is coming a time that the entire little store fronts will be closed. Leaders are appointed by God. We are accountable to lead the flock. You may think God does not see you and your sin. But pastor he does. The time is coming when all the fake ministries will be shut down. Things you did before, will not work anymore. We all must get on our knees and pray. Only the sanctified and holy will make it in the next season. You are about to be exposed. No need in crying now. You know what you have done to my people. The last will be first. The first will be last. The time is now Repent! Repent! Repent!

When you repent of your sins, there will be strategy, I will lay out for you. You know that business idea you had in your heart years ago. It will come to pass with the right strategy. Then there was several products you had on your mind to create, but never did. They will come forth my child. I will place my brilliant concepts into your mind, and you will be a producer just like your father. After all you are my child. You can do what your father has ordained you to do. Do not look toward the left or right. Just look up my child, where your help comes from above. We can do this together, if you say ok father I am tired of fighting this all by myself. I give you full reign in my life. Stomp the flesh out and take over me daddy. I trust you with my life, my will and everything I have is your father. Father with all the troubles in this world. You are needed every day for all the decision I make in my life. There is nothing I can do without my heavenly father. You lead and I will follow. Right now it may seem hard to endure my child. Taste and see it will be sweet in the end. The way has been paved for you my daughter and son a long time ago. I was just waiting for you to say yes, to my will. The more you seek me, the more I will come for you. Do not get caught up in all this worldly holiday mess my child. You know my real birth, it is placed in your heart. Seek first the kingdom and righteous, and the rest I will give to you. My child I want to resurrect you into the light. If you just give me your life, I will give it back to you. Now being resurrected can be a hard process or an easy one. If you do not fight my word, it will be easy. I want to peel off the old flesh that had you bound. My child I want to give you a makeover into my spirit realm. There you will fly high like an eagle. There will be many problems you will face in this life. When I give you my wings, you will be able to fly over all the obstacles that have been holding you back from going forward.

The season we are going through is a very trying time for most of my saints and pastors. We must try to hold our peace in the mist of the storm. We must try to not back bite each other with mean words. We seem to be having pastors, bashing churches, and pastors bashing each other and their style of preaching. (God says) enough is enough! You just preach the word, and deliver it to my people. The saints are getting tired of your bashing parties, because you don't have any scripture to recite to the people. Let my word get down in your heart. Once my word gets down in your heart, you want need any notes, because you and the word have become as one. How can my youth come in to a house that is not in order. How can I trust you with my babies, when you act like a baby yourself. The church needs to get in order, the whole world is looking at you. The people want answers! If you as pastors, bishops, teachers, don't have anything good to say about anyone, just keep your mouth shut. I am raising up a younger generation without a lot of trash in his or her truck. They will deliver the word with fire. Then there are some older saints that you have not recognized. This is the year I am calling them out of these dead churches. They will step out and do thus say it the Lord. I have to make this shift right now, before this mess gets any uglier. My children you know longer need to be afraid to just step out on faith. My children just take one step and I will take two right behind you. This is the year when you have to start that business that has been on your mind for a long time my daughter. This is the year my son when you must step out into your musical career or any other dreams you have. This is your year 2012, you must conquer all things I have put down inside of you to do. The door is open, it is your time to just jump in. No more excuses, just make it happen. The door will only be open for the first six months of the year. Then it will be closed. Now listen to my prophet!

There are certain prophets that are called that are sitting in your churches. I am calling, the Prophets to deliver my word to the people. You may not like what the prophet is saying. The word in her mouth will help the saints and give them comfort. The saints have been listening to the pastors or preachers. You have been hurting and confusing my children. It is time now for the Prophets to give the word and not sugar coat it. There is no need my son or daughter to be jealous of one another. (God says) I have called all of you to work together. This is called my body of saints. We can't have ministries that try to run the whole show by themselves. My people are tired of sitting watching reruns, after reruns. It is time for some fresh blood to take the stage. The people that sit in the back of the churches. These children are my anointed and called. This is the year they will step out into their rightful position. You will no longer use them for your own gain. Sometimes things that happen in church seem like a battle zone. The church ought not to look like the world, but it does. How can we save the world, if we do not come from out under the world. My child, do not worry about backstabbers in the church. I will handle them, from the pastor all the way down to the saints. The battle is not yours, but it is the lord's. I am shifting everything now for your good. Just be still my daughter and watch all the mess. I will show you all the ugliness behind people's motives, you have the seerer spirit my daughter, now tune in. I have called many men of God. The man of God is just not doing what I have called them to do. Today they have their own agenda, they are arrogant, and trying to run the show for their selves. The saints in the church are breaking up marriages, going after the marry men, everybody is laying with everybody. The man of god does not touch on this subject at all. This man brought his wife and children to church one week. Then the next week, I saw this so called single lady holding hands with the married man. They were all hugged up together, left church together. My sister friend said girl what do you make of that. We just have to pray for the family. I guess some of the single ladies or so desperate, they are taking the married men out of the church. It seems like today there is no shame in what people do. I feel sorry for the wife. Just like the children did back in Israel. They were hardheaded, backbiting, and stubborn, so he or she is today. The whole world is just an ugly place of turmoil. (God says) my children that are called by my name, please get on your knees and pray. We must be the watchmen of the city. When I sit back and watch this ugly stuff going on, it makes me sick to my stomach. The pastor said brings people to church. I said to myself for what. Why should we bring the street people to church, to watch this ugly show. I am in here, and I want to run, this is a mess. In order for us to bring others in, the house must be cleaned out. I put my holy oil on me and my children before we walk into the church. Then I start praying, cause there are many devils, sitting up in the poor pits. Jesus have mercy on our souls, forgive us of our sins. Some of us have lost all our morals. Where are the mothers of old times that would tell a sister how to behave. We come to church to get our praise on and dance, but we don't know how to act. A good friend of mine, once told me her husband was taken by a single lady in the church. She said the pastor did not do anything about it. They let him and his other women parade, in and out like she was his wife. She told me after this happen right in her face, she left that church and never went back. My friend said if I was in the world, I would of knew how to handle this. You never think something like this would happen in your face in church. She said my husband put me out of the house and moved his new women in my place. I just told her girl, this is a mess, I will pray for you. What he has done he will be punished for it. Just hold your peace god will see you through. The father will fight your battle for you, don't lose your faith.

This New Year the father is calling for holiness. We can't act any kind of way and think that we will be blessed. We can't live our life like a dog, and think that this is ok. Just like Jesus hung on the cross for our sins. We must pick up our cross every day and walk it out. It will not be easy. The father says if you love me, you will carry my cross. If you lose your life for me, you will gain eternity. I will give you a new life. The person you were meant to be out of your mother's womb. There is nothing but pain and sorrow in this world. My child cross over into the spirit realm, where you will have peace. You will be in this world, but not of this world. Everywhere you go my light will shine on you. There will be many people that will seek after you my child. I will give you my healing anointing. I will raise you up out of the mist of them. You will be great my child, because I have sent you into the world to make a difference. This is the year of 2012, the time of release. We must let go of the past. Have the funeral and get on with your life. We must not keep revisiting the past. Stop crying over how you miss them and you wish you had them back in your life. Stop crying over the dirt. Move on before you die of dirt. We must step into the future, let the past go and move on. So today I am having a mass funeral on what other people think. I am pronouncing that they are dead. I will go on with my life, and be happy. It is over now, and i am about to go get me some fried chicken now. God is asking us to stop, look and listen. This road map call life is meant for us to live in it. The father does not want us to live any kind of way. We are ambassadors of Christ. We must go out into the highways and byways and bring the sheep in. We are not put on this earth to just take up space. We all have a job to do, which is why God made us.

When we get busy working for the Lord, he'll get busy for us. If things in your life, do not seem like they are working out right. Maybe it is time to turn down that plate of food. It is time to go on a spiritual fast. Then the heavenly father can talk to you. When we are praying to the father, we are doing all the speaking. The father just wants to talk to you. God wants to have a relationship with us. How can you be in any type of relationship, when you do all the talking. This is the year when the father wants us to hear him. He has so much to tell you about your life. He is just waiting on you, to say I will listen. In order for God to speak to your spirit man, you must be clean on the inside. The heavenly father will not come into a dirty temple. You can cry and pray for ever, the father is not coming in to that dirt in your body. The heavenly father hates all types of sin, and some or worse than others. If you change your words, you can change your life. If you want a blessing just speak it over yourself. We can create our own atmosphere. Just like the bible says death and life is in the power of the tongue. I don't care what the doctors say about your circumstances. If you speak what you want your life to be, you will have it. We are speaking spirits. If you don't like where you are at, change your thoughts. God says once you change your thoughts you change your life. It is salvation that puts you back on your feet. Now in (Judges 5-12) is says awake, awake, oh Deborah, let Deborah O rise in you. It is time for the deborah's to take their proper place in the church. It is 2012 this is time for the Deb-o-rah's to arise and take their proper place.

My father is saying to his children, if we eat of his word daily. We will be filled up on the inside. There is no problem in our life that the word cannot solve. We have just gotten lazy. We are waiting for someone else to read the word to us. Just remember everyone word is not like you reading the word for yourself. The word affects everyone differently. It is best to try to set aside time for God. Find yourself a quiet place in your home. This way the word can slimmer down on the inside of you. Just like when you are cooking your food in the crock pot. It has to cook slowly to get done. The lord says all of the foundations of the earth are out of course. The next couple of years, will be the worst time ever. The rich man will be shut down. The world as we know it is trying to evolve in to a one world order. The next couple of years my child, try to eat off the land. There will be many wicked things happening in the world. The first thing that will be affected will be the food supply. Just like back in Moses days. We must return back to the land of our father for nourishment for your bodies. The food that is being eaten now is not good for you my child. I want to deliver you from this type of food supply. My child if you hunger and thirst after righteous you will be filled. Sometimes we have to be delivered from ourselves. We think we know everything about were the Lord is placing us or the assignment he has called us to. In order for us to know where God has assigned us, we have to ask him. No one can tell you your assignment is life but God. Sometimes we get tired of waiting for him to reveal it to us so we just act on our own. This can be the most confusing time in your life when you seek to promote yourself. If God did not say it, don't try to just run with it. The father can easily just knock you down. When your time is come, the father will first reveal it to you. Then next he will reveal it to the world. This is my child I have called. He will raise you up for all to see. Just hold on to the baby until it is time for it to be birthed out. The last stage of birth can be the most painful in your life. You are standing in the gap for all these ministries.

You are standing on the wall as a watchman. You begin to wonder, when my time will come. Why am I covering all these ministries and for what reason. I am taking all these hits, and for what reason. Then it is revealed to you. (God) has finally revealed your assignment to you. You understand why you had to wait so long. He was just getting his child ready for the Kingdom. Once you are a kingdom citizen, you are walking in authority. The heavenly father is a king and he rules in his dominion! The father came here to put rulers on earth, but we must be kingdom citizens to be able to take authority. Now the church is out of order. In order for it to flow right. We must take back our land god gave us, our Kingdom rights. The father no longer wants us to be a slave. The father does not want us to be a slave to bad habits. The father does not want us to be a slave to our pass. As he said in his word, forgetting them things that are behind us and pressing for the mark in Christ. To be Christ like is to have a kingdom mind set. Watch me change right before your eyes! There was once a caterpillar that went through the stages and turned into a butterfly. She had been trying to fly for many years. She watched all her friends flying. This little caterpillar was still eating on the word. Now that is just like a human being. When you first get the word it is like milk to you. Then as you get older you are ready for the meat. Then the closer you get to the father and summit your will. He begins to change you into what you were supposed to be in the first place. So if you are waiting for you ministry to take off, eat more word. The closer you pull toward the father. The closer the father will come to you. Today I was in this grocery store, and I heard this women singing, so anointed like a bird. She sounded better than anyone I ever heard in church. There are so many people that the father has called. They are just not walking in his calling. When this lady sang the building started to move. Everyone was just looking at her, and saying ooh, ooh! This lady was trying to cheer up another customer. God moves in great ways through anyone he wants to use.

A friend name Shirley once told me that strange things are happening in the church. She said girl did you know that the church is getting like the club now. I said no, what happening sister! Well men are giving out their phone numbers to the single ladies. Then girl they date them or have sex with them for a couple of weeks. Then they kick them to the curb! Then the men go on to the next one. Girl is this happening in your church too. Yeah girl that is happening in most of the churches, the men are going wild, cause the women are letting them make a fool out of them. Once he gets the milk, it is not guarantee he has to buy the cow. Then he just moves on. You know Shirley they have all these women conference, but I have not heard anyone ever say anything about a conference to teach young ladies how to shut their legs up. My father is calling for a holy people. It is hard to be holy and wait on the man God has for you when you are laying with everything that comes in the church. Just because they have on a suit does not make them a Christian, living for Jesus. Then Shirley some of the things they get from these men they can't get rid of. Girl we just have to pray! You right! If we don't stand in the gap who will. How can the children look up to parents when they are acting like this. Now I see why the 20 and 30 year olds are getting skipped over. My father is going after the 3 or 4 year olds. They love the Lord and are pure in spirit. We must serve the Lord in spirit and in truth. Now he is not talking about spirits you get from the liquor store. Now if your spirit is filled up with all kinds of trash. You are living your life like a gutter rat. You cannot worship the Lord in spirit and in truth. Your life is false and fake! You are just going through the motions every Sunday. Why waste your time?

God opens all kinds of doors. The first door is a physical door. The second door will only open when you use the code. If you have the right code the door will open. The third kind of door is the door of faith. The door will only open if you are close to its presence. The last kind of door is a timing door. The door only opens at a certain time. In between the time of music, the praise and worship leader has to wait for the right time to play songs. The problem with this door is if he misses the introduction then he has to wait. (Numbers 13) This year god is going to feed you something you never had. If we just fast and pray the hand of the lord is going to move on your circumstance in 2012. God has been trying to talk to you for several years. He just wants to talk to you. God wants to take you from lack to abundance, from single to married, from barrenness to fruitfulness. The father will supply all your needs, if you will just yield your life to him. (God) wants you to live a happy and fruitful life. Just like when you eat too much food, you feel miserable. When you consume too much of the trash in this world it clogs your spirit. You have to be able to minister to others with a clean spirit. If you try to minister with trash in your body, how can you tell anyone how to live when you are not an example. God just wants us to be Christ like in everything we do. Then the Holy Ghost will come through and touch people for us.

I was talking to a friend the other day, name Alice. She told me some strange stuff, that almost made my hair stand up off my back. This church she used to go too is fake. She said girl if you are down on your luck and you need help, don't ask them. Then I said girl that is hard to believe. When people call into the radio station for help they help them. She said girl please! Alice told me she asks the pastor himself if the church could help her out and he said no! It's like they put on a mask to the general public. Then when they take the mask off it is scary and ugly. So I told my friend Alice I know how she feels, other people have mentioned this place before. Some churches run God house like a business. If you don't have anything to invest in the house, they are not going to do anything for you anyway. My friend Alice gave her tides every week. How can you speak in public about you have a heart for people and stab your fellow saint in the back. I just told my friend God will not be mock. They will pay for what they did to her and other saints, just sit back and watch the house crumble down. This year 2012 it will be more shaking and rooting out of fake people. How can you talk about some saints that don't work and or lazy, when you don't work yourself. Some pastors expect the saints to pay their mortgage payments for them and buy them a car. They don't care how the saints make it as long as their family is taken care of. The devil is a liar. When no one in the church is prospering but the preacher, you may just want to take a closer look. Look at all the automobiles in the lot outside are they old. What types of clothing are the people wearing in the church. If the only person that is dress up is the pastor, you might want to take a closer look. If the word is being delivered as thus say the lord, the money will come to you. Some people are so greedy for money till they can't see past their noise. When all the shaking is over with only the righteous houses will be standing. The ugly mess that some of the pastors have done to their members is about to be reviled to the world. (God) sees all that you have done, and he says repent, repent, repent, of your sins. How can you preach my world, when you are boastful and proud. I will no longer stand for you hurting my children. When someone else is delivering a word, you get jealous and take the mike from them. You wonder why your ministry has not gone any further than it has. I'll tell you why, you are not humble, you are conceded, and you are arrogant! Until you repent of your sins you want go too far at all. The only nation you are going to is the one in your mind. If my people who are called by my name would humble themselves and pray! (God) says, if my people who are called by my name would humble themselves and pray! Then another friend name Rebecca told me about her church. What is going on. They are making all the members in the choir sign a contract stating they would pay their tides each week, and show up at choir rehearsal. They have to sign a contract or they get kick out of the choir. I just told my friend this is not right. God does not like ugly! Rebecca said I guess they are trying to get that other part of the day care paid for. This is why many people are not coming in the churches anymore. They are acting too much like people of the world. You cannot tell the difference anymore. If makes you think to yourself, and you say when I was in the world I had to fight. I did not know that in the church, from the head on down you have to continue to fight the saints. (God) says my child just be still I will fight your battle for you. He is a mighty God! My child I will place you in better surrounding, where there are people that love you. Just ask me my child! Tell me where it hurts and I will take care of it. His eyes are open wide to everything that is happening in the church. Just when you think he does not see your mess the almighty God sees all.

CPSIA information can be obtained
at www.ICGtesting.com
Printed in the USA
BVHW082017070922
646441BV00003B/506